JUSTIN CRAIG LaCOUR

THE TOP FOUR ONLINE SURVEY SITES

GET PAID FOR SURVEYS IN 2017

JUSTIN CRAIG LaCOUR

Copyright © 2016 by JUSTIN CRAIG LaCOUR

All rights reserved. No part of this publication may be reproduced, distributed or transmitted in any form or by any means, without prior written permission from the author.

TABLE OF CONTENTS

DEDICATION iv
CHAPTER 1 5
    The Top Four Online Survey Sites 5
CHAPTER 2 9
    Global Test Market 9
CHAPTER 3 13
    Survey Savvy 13
CHAPTER 4 18
    Opinion Outpost 18
CHAPTER 5 20
    Inbox Dollars 20
CONCLUSION 24

DEDICATION

I dedicate this book to my wife and kids. I love you!

CHAPTER 1

The Top Four Online Survey Sites

There are several online survey sites but some of them ask too much of you and your time for pennies. The survey sites that I'm going to share with you are going to give you the opportunity to make money for years. In 2013, I was introduced to online surveys. I have been taking online surveys for four years and the earning potential is unlimited. The more surveys you complete, the more money you earn.

It takes a lot of time to take online surveys, so you have to be dedicated in the process. Some survey sites will offer you a survey and only pay you $0.25 for an hour survey. There are hundreds of online survey companies out there but they do not compare to the top four that I'm going to share with you. I would not quit my day job because you are not going to be rich completing online surveys. I make an average

THE TOP FOUR ONLINE SURVEY SITES: GET PAID FOR SURVEYS IN 2017

of $300 to $400 a month with online surveys. I'm not going to share the top ten surveys with you because I only have experience with the four and those are the ones I will share with you. There are a lot of books that list the top 10 survey sites but I doubt if they actually receive money from each of those sites that they are sharing with their readers. One of the companies that I am going to share with you, also offers focus groups as part of their survey site.

These focus groups average from $100 to $225 for a 2-3 hour focus group. I really hope that you take advantage of this opportunity because it would be nice and relieving to see multiple deposits going to your PayPal account every week. It is also nice to receive survey checks in the mail. You should see the look on the bank teller's face when I show up at the bank with 10 survey checks and the teller is wondering what's going on. Then she asks me if this is a joke because the survey checks are colorful and don't look like traditional checks that people write every day. I explained to her that they are online survey checks and she was surprised to see that she could potentially get paid to complete online surveys in her spare time. She deposited my 10 survey checks into my checking account and asked me how she could sign up for the survey sites. A lot of people are not familiar with online surveys and the ones that have heard about them think that they are a scam. Paid surveys are not a scam. Well, at least the top four that I am going to share with you are legitimate sites that are accredited by the Better Business Bureau. I know this because I have been getting paid to complete online surveys since 2013.

THE TOP FOUR ONLINE SURVEY SITES: GET PAID FOR SURVEYS IN 2017

CHAPTER 2

Global Test Market

The first On-line survey site that pays you in points is Global Test Market. You will accumulate points or sweepstakes entries for each survey that you complete. The site will also screen you out during the initial process if you do not qualify for that particular survey. I complete surveys everyday on this site because they continuously send you more and more surveys as you complete them.

The surveys are usually worth 30 to 35 points but sometimes you will receive surveys worth 50 and 100 points, depending on the topic. Once you receive around 1100 points that equates to approximately $50 in a PayPal deposit. The higher paid surveys are usually in the intelligence and computer based fields. Some of the surveys take 10 minutes and some can take up to 30 minutes, depending on the amount of points that the survey is worth. There is a minimum $50 worth of points that must be accumulated before you can request a payout to PayPal. Once the money is available in your PayPal, they will send you an e-mail to the e-mail account that you have on file.

Global Test Market also sends surveys to your e-mail address daily and as you complete more surveys, they will send you more surveys to complete. The site offers product testing that they will send to your mailing address. Once you test the product, you will receive a follow up survey to complete the process and then you are awarded points for your time in the testing. I have tested several products over the last 3 years with the site. They also have surveys that you can complete on your mobile phone. I usually complete these surveys when I am waiting in line at the barbershop or at the store. You will be surprised on how much time you waste on social media. Every time that I have a few minutes to spare, I log on to the computer to complete a few surveys. The points add up fast and before you know it, it is time to request another $50 PayPal payment.

Keep in mind that you will have to file taxes if you make at least $600 with the site during the calendar year. I have made YouTube videos on my YouTube channel to share online surveys with everyone but most people don't believe that they can make money online especially with these type of surveys. It is 2017, and the most successful companies conduct their businesses online. Please take advantage of Global Test Market and sign up today, because this is an easy way to earn more money in your spare time. Remember to keep your day job, because this is just a supplemental income.

THE TOP FOUR ONLINE SURVEY SITES: GET PAID FOR SURVEYS IN 2017

CHAPTER 3

Survey Savvy

The second survey site that I want to share with you is Survey Savvy. This site is unique because it offers online surveys and focus groups. They also offer you to test products that they will send to your house. After you have completed your product analysis, the site will send you a follow up survey. Once the follow up survey is complete, the site will credit your account with certain amount of dollar. It takes a while for you to get credit for your surveys but you will be compensated for your efforts.

I remember checking my account one day and it had jumped from $10 to over $100 from surveys I had completed weeks earlier. The surveys do not take too long to complete and the check is mailed to the address that you have on file. It takes approximately 2-4 weeks for the money to arrive to your address but it is very dependable. You can request the money in your account with as little as $1 in your account. I remember requesting my first check, which was only $5 but once I received the check, I knew that it was a legitimate company and that it was real.

There are still thousands of people who believe that you cannot make money with online surveys and that is why I always keep a survey check in my wallet to show friends and family that this is a legitimate opportunity they can't afford to miss. Some of them have started to complete surveys online and some do not take the time to explore new opportunities. They waste 3 to 4 hours a day on social media, whereas, they could be spending that time completing surveys and earning extra income. If you complete online surveys long enough, you feel unproductive when you are wasting time online or hanging out with friends. The site also sends out several surveys and some are worth $25 to $50. The higher paying surveys are rare but they are available. Once it is offered you have to complete the survey right away because it will be completed by the competition if you wait too long.

This company has the highest earning potential due to the fact that they offer focus group opportunities. If you meet the minimum requirements for a focus group, the site will send you an e-mail asking if you are interested in the focus group. The focus groups average from $100 to $225 for a 2-3 hour focus group. Once you receive the e-mail invitation, you will have to call the company to apply for the focus group. I have been screened out of a lot of $100 focus groups and it was really painful to miss out on the opportunity. When you are screened out, they will ask you if you know anyone who may fit the criteria. I have personally recommended someone to a focus group and they received $100 in cash for a 2 hour focus group. The focus groups are only available in specific locations and the site will give you the details if you are eligible to participate. Please get started today, and you will not regret becoming a member of the Survey Savvy team.

JUSTIN CRAIG LaCOUR

CHAPTER 4

Opinion Outpost

The third survey site that offers a PayPal pay option is Opinion Outpost. This site sends out surveys daily, ranging from $0.50 to $5.50. You can only complete 5 surveys within 12 hours. So I usually average around $10 a day, which equates to around $300 a month. Your money is deposited directly into your PayPal account. You can also choose to receive an Amazon.com or an ITunes gift card. The bonus with this site is the fact that the site has a $40,000 year-long cash give away. Every time a member takes a survey, they are selected into the quarterly drawing for a chance to win $10,000.

I have been with them for four years, so hopefully I will get to win the quarterly prize one day. This site has new survey opportunities every day. They will also ask you if you are interested in specific studies to earn extra money. It is very easy to sign up for an account and you can start completing surveys in your spare time. If you do not have an internet connection, you can always go to Starbucks, McDonalds, public library and any other place with a free high speed internet connection. The surveys work better with high speed internet, due to the types of surveys that are offered by the site.

If you don't have high speed internet, the surveys will take a long time to load from page to page and you will be discouraged from completing the survey. There is no purchase necessary to join the site and it is free. The site is open to all 50 United States that are eligible to participate on a Survey Sampling International panel and meet the age requirement for such particular panel.

CHAPTER 5

Inbox Dollars

The fourth survey site is Inbox Dollars. This site offers several ways to make money. There is an initial process where the site will pay you when you first sign up. I always elect to receive payment by check and the minimum before payout is $30. You can earn money on this site by completing surveys, watching videos, reading e-mails, referring others, playing games, and there is also a Spin and Win Wheel that you get to spin up to 25 times a day to win cash and survey tokens.

I have personally won $5 twice spinning the wheel on this site. The site usually gives you sweepstakes entries for spinning the wheel. Another way to earn money with the site is to use Inbox Dollars to conduct your daily searches. Most people use Google, Bing, or Yahoo to conduct their daily searches but those sites do not pay you cash to use their sites. With the Inbox Dollars search tool, you can earn up to $0.15 a day on qualified searches and a $0.05 search royalty reward for any week that you are able to search for four or more days. I know it seems like a lot but you are going to conduct online searches anyway, so why not get paid for it? The surveys take longer to complete than the other three sites and you will only receive a small amount of money for your time.

On the average, it takes about 4 to 5 weeks to earn $30 if you are completing surveys part-time. There is a $3.00 processing fee per payment request. I don't really agree with a $3.00 processing fee per payment request but that is their policy. The check takes approximately 10 to 16 days to cycle through the verification process and then it can be issued and sent to you through the United States Postal Service. Another payment option that is available is to receive payment through

THE TOP FOUR ONLINE SURVEY SITES: GET PAID FOR SURVEYS IN 2017

Visa cash card. Once you receive the check in the mail, it is a validation that this is real and the site is legitimate. I always keep a survey check in my wallet so that I can encourage friends and family to join me online. I always work on the other three survey sites first and save Inbox Dollars for last due to the time it takes to complete one survey.

Some surveys take 10 minutes and some can take over 30 minutes to complete for $0.50. The great thing about all of these survey sites is that you can complete them while you are watching television or waiting in line at the post office. One day I was at the barbershop waiting on a haircut and I decided to complete some online surveys on my smartphone while I waited on my appointment. I was able to complete enough surveys to pay for my haircut and the tip by the time I sat in the barber chair.

Time is money and every moment counts. Most people in North America spend over an hour a day on social media. Sometimes, I realize I have been on social media for too long with over two hours gone already and I have not accomplished anything that will increase my cash flow.

CONCLUSION

In conclusion, there are four online sites that can provide anyone with $300 to $400 of additional income every month. It is supplemental income and it is not meant to replace your full time job. You can use the extra money to make a car payment, pay your cell phone, or utility bill. There are hundreds of online survey sites but they all offer something different. Several survey sites ask you to buy products in order to complete their surveys. The four survey sites that I have shared with you do not require you to buy anything, which is the right way to do business.

If a survey site asks you to purchase something in order to complete a survey or study, it is not a legitimate survey site. If you sign up for the sites that I have shared with you and you have a computer and high speed internet connection, you will be able to complete online surveys

24 hours a day, seven days a week. Please step out of your comfort zone and sign up for the top four survey sites that I have shared with you and you will thank me later. I'll see you online!

www.ingramcontent.com/pod-product-compliance
Lightning Source LLC
Chambersburg PA
CBHW031601210526
45464CB00003B/1384